T0209785

ALSO BY RAMESH SHARMA

AMERICA TATTWAMASI
AMERICA ARISE AND AWAKE

AMERICA
THY SIMMERING
AGONY

RAMESH SHARMA

authorHOUSE®

AuthorHouse™
1663 Liberty Drive
Bloomington, IN 47403
www.authorhouse.com
Phone: 1 (800) 839-8640

Published by AuthorHouse 10/16/2019

ISBN: 978-1-7283-3205-5 (sc)
ISBN: 978-1-7283-3204-8 (e)

Print information available on the last page.

"The day will come when my prana will be integrated into the vast space, and my physical body reduced to ashes.

At that very moment of reckoning, O America, what shall I have to remember, if I now consciously fail to speak the truth?

Therefore, O paragon of freedom and liberty, pray allow me to reveal the truth."

Excerpt from **America Arise And Awake**

CONTENTS

POIGNANT TEARS

I don't see sin in being born as a human. Rather I see sin in keeping mum when it comes to resisting evil. I see sin in tolerance toward assaults on freedom and liberty. I see sin in connivance at attempts to decimate human conscience.

I don't want to blame anyone, nor do I want to incriminate any party or organization. However the bitter truth is that our national politics seems to have almost touched the nadir.

In sharp contrast to lofty values and great ideals enshrined in our Constitution and the Declaration of Independence, our politics seems to be obsessed with sleazy smear, inveterate vengeance and ceaseless retribution.

Most unfortunately, the core Being of this great nation has been the first victim. No less victimized are the American people, and their trust and confidence in sprawling democratic institutions. Those who have even a scintilla of love towards this great nation can easily hear the groan of her aching Soul.

This book is a modest attempt at giving expression to the voice of our collective conscience. Although some of my words might sound blunt, pungent and brusque to some, they are the gospels of my heart, ventilated with malice towards none.

America and her ideals, based on the Upanishadic doctrine of Universality of Spirit, carry preternatural attributes, capable of transcending both time and space. Freedom, liberty and democracy are the life and soul of this great nation.

Let us hope, the ominous aberration facing our national politics today is nothing but a bad dream, ephemeral and transient. Let us look forward to a new day when all Americans - irrespective of ideology, race, religion, color, creed, gender and ethnicity - will unitedly march ahead under the Star Spangled Banner. And the immortal ideals of democracy, freedom and liberty will be upheld with exceptional American spirit.

There is always a symbiotic relation between literature and the society we live in. My poems are poignant tears, shed over the agony and torture our country is going through. If they could provide even a sense of succor to our anguished present, I will with utmost humility take it as a great tribute to my endeavor.

Ramesh Sharma
Massachusetts, USA
October, 2019

NATIONAL ANTHEM

O America,
The divine rendezvous,
Where compassion trysts with strength,
And beauty with power.

An iridescent dream
Of all race, religion,
Ethnicity, creed and color.

O paragon of freedom and liberty,
The cherished horizon,
Where humanity meets the Almighty.

Thy air, space, rivers,
Mountains, plateaus and prairies
All exuding the empyrean fragrance
Of universality of spirit.

Thy soul reverberating
With the melody of 'We the People',
O America,
We take refuge in thee.

Sole hope of humans and humanity,
O America,
To the last drop of our blood,
We pledge to fight for thy honor, dignity,
Independence and sovereignty.

Raising the glorious Star Spangled Banner,
Freedom and liberty shall we spread
Across the earth and the space.

Hail to thee, America,
The manifestation of
Grandeur, majesty and grace!

Authentic definition of
Truth, order, justice,
Prosperity, and harmony,
O America,
Thou art the most coveted
Abode of the brave.

O divine soul of humanity,
We prostrate before thee,
And pay our deepest obeisance:
America,
Tattwamasi, tattwamasi, tattwamasi!

THIS IS CALIFORNIA!

Come on everybody from all corners of the world
This is California!
'A house that provides shelter to all who need it
    and sanctuary to all who seek it'
A coveted paradise of immigrants from across the
    globe
An idyllic destination
A proud Sanctuary State

Dear immigrants,
You are most welcome, regardless of your past
    history
Guided by the great mission of 'California for all',
    we are here to extend our good wishes and
    warm regards to you all
You will find entire America now reverberating
    with this great spirit, courtesy of our
    comrades-in-arms across the country

Even if you have committed felonies, we don't care
You are free to do whatever you want to, here in
    this land of immigrants
Your past crimes will not be allowed to preclude
    you from walking freely in our communities
Because you are the most privileged ones, even
    above the law of the land
Don't worry about your livelihood

People of this country are more than eager to toil
full 24 hours to support and sustain you

If necessary, we will manage to collect adequate
funds, even by levying taxes on our people

Because we command their trust and confidence
as 'prudent stewards of taxpayer dollars'

They will generously contribute to free health
benefits for you, and members of your family

You shouldn't bother about the future of your
children, too

Their education will be entirely free

Worried about housing?

That isn't any issue

You can accommodate yourselves anywhere,
including our parks, sidewalks, and public
places

You are free to use our streets and sidewalks as
substitutes for lavatories

Our sidewalks and train stations are strewn
with surfeit of disposable items, including
syringes and ragged clothes, visibly relating
to narcotic drugs and illicit substances

However, we are more focused on the
transcendental pleasure the inhabitants
of this state are entitled to, than on those
seemingly unwelcome paraphernalia

As far as the soaring homeless epidemic in this
state is concerned, you need not bother about

it, too. It won't in any way undercut our
cordiality towards you
You need not fret about the issue of sanitation
That is not your problem, we will take care of that
We just want to make sure that you are comfortable
and happy, along with your family here
Don't forget to bring your friends and relatives into
this land of opportunity as soon as you are
settled here
If you have any problems preparing necessary
documents, however fake, just let's know
We have legions of attorneys and experts to
skillfully address your concerns
They know how to turn each and every loophole
of the system to your best advantage

Whether you are a gang member or an agent of
some drug cartel, it should not bother us a bit
You are most welcome
Our border is always open for you and the likes
To make sure that you will always be treated as such,
we have unleashed a sustained campaign to
decimate entire law enforcement apparatus
of ours
We hate our law enforcement authorities because
of their xenophobic resistance to your influx
They say you are entering illegally, and therefore
your presence in this country is not acceptable

They say criminal elements, with the aim of committing crimes, enter through porous borders

Even dreaded terrorists of ISIS and the likes might conveniently exploit this opportunity and cause unimaginable harm to America and its people

They claim that there is a crisis in our Southern border in the wake of migrant caravans from several countries trying to make inroads into US

We are diametrically opposed to their position

It is our principled stand that America is made up of immigrants, and therefore its borders should never be closed to anyone who wants to come into this country

We want as many people as possible to enter this country, and therefore we strongly advocate an open border

Whoever ventures into this country must be granted political asylum, no matter whether someone admits to having been henpecked or beaten up by the spouse

We believe, it is totally unfair to deny immigrants - no matter whatever their status - voting rights, once they are in this country

The incumbent administration claims that they, along with members of various cartels and gangs, are a threat to the safety and security of America and the American people

How ludicrous a claim!

We have never heard any leaders of political parties complain about the infringement of high walls, protecting their mansions

Again they blame the immigrants for the death of tens of thousands of Americans every year on account of illicit drugs

What a concocted hoax!

Has any member of both Houses of Parliament ever reported the members of their families having been killed by the consumption of narcotics and related substances?

Equally disgusting is their claim that the members of violent gangs such as MS13 are responsible for the rape and murder of Americans

This, too, seems totally inconsistent with what our respectable elites have experienced so far

These are primarily some of the reasons why we have chosen to mock their divisive, bigoted and racist 'wall-building project' by offering to contribute not more than $1

We believe, closing borders, especially for what they call illegal immigrants, is absolutely immoral

It is against the letter and spirit of both our Constitution and the Declaration of Independence

Not only that, even the use of 'illegal' for those who stealthily sneak into our country is unacceptable to us

The crisis they are so passionately referring to is nothing but a 'manufactured' one

Whatever we might have said in the past in favor of a secure and closed border, we don't have any qualm in staging an about-face

It is our firm conviction that consistency in politics is a moronic proposition

Machiavellian opportunism must be adopted as the best credo by our party organization, we maintain

You might certainly feel exulted to learn that we have openly likened (Immigration and Customs Enforcement) ICE to the infamous KKK in order to foil its law enforcement efforts

You need not worry about their activities, aimed at securing the borders of this country

Strategically enough, we have blamed the accidental death of some migrant children, too, on our incumbent racist administration

Seizing on our majority in the House, we are planning to enact legislations that promote your interests over racist, parochial and nationalist policies of this administration

We are determined to 'offer an alternative to the corruption and incompetence in the White House'

We are really encouraged by surreptitious and tacit
    support of some disgruntled collaborators,
    even from our rival organization
We feel immensely honored to announce that
    history has chosen us to give a new direction
    to this country of immigrants
We have come to realize that values and institutions
    this country has hitherto stood for, have
    become completely obsolete
Therefore, we are trying to radically redefine
    the basic premises that govern our judicial,
    political, social and cultural systems

We have been strongly advocating the policy of
    squeezing the wealthy
We maintain that by creating enormous wealth
    for themselves, they have committed crimes
    against majority of the people who are poor
    and deprived
We are not even in a position to acknowledge their
    contribution, if there is any, to the economic
    prosperity and wellbeing of our nation,
    because generating wealth is in itself a sin
Some sort of punitive actions must be taken against
    them, so nobody will dare embark on the
    same kind of pursuit in future

We have always taken it as an imperial conceit for
    this country to claim itself exceptional

We want to carve out a new international order
where America, too, will always stand at par
with some third world countries of Asia or
some banana republics of Latin America

Scores of people from prominent bureaucratic
positions have pledged to clandestinely
support us in advancing our cause

We are no less fortunate in being blessed with
the entire weight, some prominent political
figures have decided to throw behind us

Bruised and lacerated as they are by the unexpected
twists of events, they seem inclined to
console themselves by actively contributing
to our agendas

We have also evolved a tacit understanding of not
recognizing the incumbent administration's
accomplishments - no matter how stupendous

We are at all cost determined to sabotage the so-
called mission of Making America Great Again

We believe, it is nothing but an abhorrent anathema

We don't want to belittle other countries and
peoples of the world, by harboring such a
nationalistic mission

Pursuant to the policy of deflecting the incumbent
administration's attention from its racist,
xenophobic and nationalist agendas, we
are trying to keep it bogged down in a
series of endless inquiries, subpoenas and
investigations

It is most unfortunate not only for us, but also for entire Americans that the Mueller Investigation turned out to be a ludicrous fiasco, much to the detriment of our noble pursuit

We are, however, confident that the dissipation of tens of millions of dollars in tax payers' money won't bother the American public who seem long inured to politicians' vile practices

Truly speaking, we have a new vision for the future of America and the Americans

It is with this grand vision in mind that we had enunciated a great doctrine of 'leading from behind'

In what our adversaries have unjustifiably tried to misconstrue as a sellout, we had agreed to substantially reduce our defense capability, too, with a view to resetting our relations with Russia

We had even propped up Iran by granting it exceptionally huge amount of cash in the hope of bringing regional balance of power on an even keel

Longstanding pampering on the part of some US administrations has prompted countries like Israel and Saudi Arabia to act as deviant bullies - a reality that must be changed

We are intuitively convinced that the acquisition of nuclear weapons by Islamic Iran, however deceptively, will ultimately contribute to the creation of an equitable global order, virtually based on our vision in relation to the highly volatile region of Middle East

We are not interested in rocking the boat when it comes to our relations with China whose generosity, like that of Russia, has always made us immensely enriched, rather in an inscrutable way

We are trying to apply a timely brake on the relentless advancement of science and technology to prevent them from precipitating 'apocalyptic climate change'

Therefore, we have envisioned a new America, determined to dispense with achievements, however wondrous, of the past, including airplanes, big buildings, architectural marvels, and sprawling establishments

Out of sincere concern for the health of our fellow countrymen, we are even considering enacting laws that enforce rationing of their daily diets

Opposition to corporate interests as well as concern for the preservation of environment might force us to issue some decree of sorts, enjoining Americans to strictly pursue veganism

You might be exhilarated to learn, particularly
about our commitment to the health and
overall advancement of women

We are prepared to go to the extent of sanctioning
infanticide, when it comes to protecting
women's rights to control over their own
body, even outdoing the Chinese mothers
who would surreptitiously throw their
female babies into the well, just to avoid
being prosecuted by the draconian one-child
policy of the totalitarian communist regime

Equally committed we are to the creation of a
socio-cultural order that bestows upon our
women immense power to vanquish toxic
masculinity

Meantime, as a nation committed to lofty values
and principles, it is imperative that we
embark upon deep soul-searching and quiet
introspection

We must be sincere to our own conscience and
acknowledge the responsibility for having
decisively contributed to the downfall and
disintegration of former Soviet Union, truly
a socialist haven, and a perennial source of
inspiration for entire working class people
across the globe

We believe, our movement aimed at actively
resisting and defying the Federal
Government in all sectors - beginning from

law enforcement and immigration - will ultimately pave the ground for our total liberation, thereby allowing us to establish a proud socialist homeland of our own

Likewise, in keeping with our abiding commitment to the epic vision of 'letting hundred flowers bloom', we inspire all states of America to flourish and blossom in full freedom and independence

Once our mission is accomplished, it will not only usher in a new era in global politics, but also serve as atonement for having convulsed international peace and order, by consigning a peaceable empire to the ash heap of history

That the foundation of this country itself was fraught with endemic racism, has made us feel more urgent to launch into some transformational pursuit, so we can rectify gross mistakes committed in the past

There are several instances when America had committed enormities in foreign lands - crimes that, we believe, should not go unpunished, in one way or another

As a first step in this direction, we are developing some sort of collusion with such elements as are not only falsely alleged to be anti-semitic, but also rightly critical of the 'massacre' carried out by this country in the past

Denunciation of Jews and the Zionist state of Israel vis-a-vis Arab and Muslim countries of the Middle East will certainly be a salient feature of our foreign policy proposition

We are seriously considering developing some sort of solidarity, however surreptitious, with couple of organizations that view religion and politics, exclusively in extremist and fanatical terms

This is in keeping with our policy of coopting vibrant and daring international organizations, regardless of their radical propensity and predispositions

We won't hesitate to pour fire and brimstones on anyone who does disagree with us, so none will dare criticize our policies in future

Hollywood's unqualified enthusiasm in playing second fiddle to our *avant garde* philosophy has further emboldened us towards realizing our goals

It is our policy of making the maximum utilization of mainstream media, as well as entire social media outlets that won't hesitate even to hurl expletives at our rivals and their supporters

We highly appreciate their unalloyed obsequiousness, and the exceptional expertise in concocting stories, which serve to bolster the best interests of America and the American people

Ours is not the policy of directly fomenting
violence, but should it occur somewhere in
our interest, we won't hesitate to wink at

Some who claim to be in majority, extoll the
legacies of so-called moderate democrats
such as, Woodrow Wilson, Franklin D.
Roosevelt, Harry S. Truman and Kennedy,
and choose to frown upon us as nothing, but
an aberrant fringe group, estranged from the
mainstream
They seem more in league with our opponents
whose vainglorious celebration of the
US Constitution and the Declaration of
Independence invariably tends to undermine
our goal
Therefore, it is imperative that we seamlessly
navigate the hurdles and hindrances posed
both by the rival organization, and our own
so-called mainstreamers

Dear fellow immigrants,
It is indisputable that the world is going to end
in 12 years because of apocalyptic climate
change
Therefore, there is absolutely no point in giving
birth to children, too
Efforts at further perpetuating human species do
not make any sense

Years leading up to the end of our planet, along
with human species, are certainly going to be
unbearably traumatic, particularly because of
deplorable forces' racist, xenophobic, bigoted
and nationalistic outlook

Could it be an alternative solution that we all
respond to the echo, hitherto reverberating
around the Heaven's Gate?

Who knows, Empyrean Destination might be
impatiently awaiting our heroic arrivals!

Maybe even today, Bo, from some corner of
California is beckoning to us all!

March, 2019

SATYAMEWA JAYATE!

Infatuated by enticing offerings of the Sanctuary State of California, a gentleman in his mid thirties, apparently persecuted by some fanatical religious authority in a distant land, once landed in the city of San Francisco through due process of law. Although he was a graduate with Eastern Philosophy as his major, he could not find a job that would exactly fit his disposition, temperament and aptitude.

Following a euphoric hiatus of a couple of months, the man, as he was profoundly influenced by chromatic vistas, presented by the hippie movement of the 1960s, began to plunge steadily into the dark world of alcohol and narcotics. The more he would dive into the world of illicit substances, the more he believed he could find an escape from his burgeoning predicaments.

Not surprisingly, policies and programs of the Sanctuary City would, in one way or another, further inspire him to hurtle towards his unbelievably enchanting 'phantasmagoric world of Nirvana'.

Within a relatively short span of time, like
thousands of other unfortunates, inhabiting
the city, he did predictably end up being one
of the most welcome guests of City of San
Francisco sidewalks that would caress him
with a ragtag tent, and some 'psychedelic'
substances, along with their sordid
paraphernalia.

Stripped of basic honor and dignity of life, thanks
to the boastful and high sounding rhetoric
of so-called Sanctuary State authorities, he
was once overheard mumbling from inside
the tiny tent.

However obfuscatory, discursive and disjointed,
apparently due to the consumption of some
narcotic substances, his pronouncements
were in essence an elegy to democracy,
freedom and liberty - much cherished
values, as if the decimation of which he were
strongly resenting.

Although expertly flavored with scientific and
philosophical spice, his words were no less a
caveat to the authorities that he believed were
bent on making a travesty of our Constitution
and the Declaration of Independence.

Tumescent rivers crisscrossing my body strive to
defy their limits.

My brain - corporeal abode of sun, moon and
stars - sinks into eternal passivity.

Nudity of Nature dances to the vibe of rock and
jazz in the discotheque of my heart.

My conscience turns out to be a brothel where
whores of different hues try to quench lewd
thirst of reprobates, libertines and roués.

Morality, ethics and principles are subjected to water
boarding. Acid poured into the eyes of public.

Atmospherics - ornately adorned by the cataclysmic
waltzes of rockets, mortars, grenades and
drones - slide into surrealistic chimera.

Violently upstaged humanity appalled at the
diabolic tantrums, thrown by corporeal
specters and apparitions.

Apocryphal legends, legacies and epics of Gods
and Goddesses are unmasked.

Cultures and civilizations seized by
anthropomorphic impulses, reverberating
in the brain of androids.

Jewels of creation, youths, fervently hankering
after opioids and narcotic drugs.

Suffering diminished testosterone, they turn
misogynist, and start loathing Rambha,
Tilottama, and Urvashi.

Amorous beauty of Nature bemoans the ascetic
indifference of atavistic aficionados that
revel in inscrutable stoicism.

The world is a competition between libido and impotence, attraction and repulsion, compassion and hatred, and altruism and selfishness.

I represent a tiny window into the vast universe. I am an enigmatic microcosm, a Delphic complexity.

Umpteen times, I have swallowed the entire creation of God. Umpteen times, I have disgorged them.

Every time they enter my body they achieve moksha, by being one with the Absolute.

Driven by erratic senses, and possessed with desires, humans morph into bestial ignoramuses.

Ignorance leads to darkness, ignorance leads to pogroms, ignorance leads to holocausts.

Ignorance is the perfect recipe for the emergence of *ubermensch*.

The root of destruction stems from darkness that relishes symbiotic relation with ignorance.

Sacred mantra of *vox populi vox dei* gets interred at the ubiquity of ignorance, passivity and darkness.

Arise and awake! O my fellow beings, what is it that has so benighted you? Haven't you seen my plight?

How can you condone the quiescence that is leading you to an infernal abyss?

Your dignity and honor has been speciously trampled, and your self esteem pulverized.

Beware! You might be reduced to a tiny cog meant to serve the nefarious design of a totalitarian machine.

Isn't it suicidal to let antibodies be defeated by insidious attacks of antigens?

Beware of the forces that unleash antigens. They are the enemies that destroy your lives.

I am freedom, I am liberty, and this is what has defined my divinity.

I have sustained this earth. I have sustained this universe. I am the definition of the cosmos.

I am the bewildering enigma, underlying the Nature of Reality.

Well, it might sound insane to you, right?

Try to go deep into your own Being. Then you will understand what I mean by these pronouncements.

If you still have some doubt, please take some trouble to foray into the brains of scientists and philosophers like Shankaracharya, Einstein and Stephen Hawking.

My fellow beings, wherever I see life I see you, whether it be on earth or in any distant corner of the universe.

Don't think that I am trying to incommode you by splashing my misfortune across your seemingly exhilarating world.

O divine entity, how can you be fooled by the allure of heavenly paradise, lusty caressing of sensual virgins, and the asinine delusion of turning a martyr.

Tear down the curtain of fatal illusions. Try to reflect on scriptures, and be blessed with their true perspectives.

I don't understand. Is it that I have gone too high today? What is it that has rendered the atmosphere so abstruse?

How come Indras, Baruns, Maruts and Agnis all seem to have been seized by paranoia, absurdity and psychosis?

O my God! How can one imagine prodding humans into eating human flesh? And that, too, in the empyrean land of freedom and liberty!

Is anyone out there who can explain to me whether we are marching towards the Kingdom of God, or retreating to the age of hunting?

O fanaticism and bigotry, why are you assaulting our psyche? Why do you want to see us reduced to wretched worms wiggling potentially under the demonic boots of some blood thirsty Helmsman?

O Golden City, California, how miserable thy plight is! Why is thy glitter waning so fast? I really feel like crying when I see thee mired in the hypocritical illusion of some fringe elements.

Who knows? The socialist streak striving to devour thy body politic might one day turn this land of the free and brave into a Gulag Archipelago?

O California, how unfortunate thou art! Thou might forever be blemished for having potentially pioneered the slide of this paradise into a hell!

O my beloved California, I know how deeply anguished thou art. Constantly aches my heart at thy silent cry.

And this is what drives me further into the world of substances, no matter how illusory and pernicious.

May God bless thee with extraordinary power and strength to resist the forces that believe in the decimation of human Soul.

I find myself stricken by conscience when I see the superb artistry of Hollywood devolve into vicious insinuations and innuendoes.

I can hardly bear the trauma that I find inflicted on my Self, when people's representatives rejoice in digging the grave of values and institutions, our beloved motherland fondly cherishes.

My pain gets completely intolerable when even some presidential hopefuls, apparently in a bid to please some unseen powers, portray this country as evil.

O my dear substances, were it not for your grace, I wouldn't be able to regurgitate these dark truths, completely oblivious to potential intimidation and violent attacks from those who fail to agree with me.

Oh, I am really confused! Am I living in the United States or some other communist dictatorship where freedom of speech is strictly prohibited?

Why do I seem overtaken by this trepidation, a phenomenon commonly found among ordinary people in totalitarian regimes, that tend to use vigilantes to suppress the voice of dissent?

No problem. Talking passionately about the true nature of our Being, the Upanishads declare that we are Brahman - eternal, infinite and imperishable. Nothing can destroy us. Really a transcendental consolation!

O my fellow beings, yield not to division and divisiveness. Bigotry and fanaticism serve none. Rise above petty parochialism.

Entire world is but one family.

Love it, rear it, nurture it. Were it not for you, O my fellow Americans, devious and callous machinations of Shani, Rahu and Ketu would have already destroyed this world.

No wonder, Yama is astounded by the prodigy, Nachiketa. The supremo of death seems completely psyched out.

Immortality triumphs. We are all Nachiketas. We all possess his preternatural attributes.

We represent the fullness. We are full. Even nukes can't destroy our fullness.

We are freedom, we are liberty. Freedom can't be incarcerated, and liberty can never be muzzled.

No veil shall be allowed to obscure the beauty of our commitment to values humane. Even an inkling of defiance will ignite a massive resistance.

We represent both mass and energy. We are interchangeable, depending on the need of time and space.

Even if we are subtracted from ourselves, we remain the same. Even if our fullness is breached, it will be replenished in no time.

Believe it or not, I have had an epiphany. The day will come when the scientific world will recognize *Brahman* as the fundamental basis of quantum theory of gravity that incorporates both general theory of gravity and quantum physics.

The flag of freedom and liberty will always be held aloft.

Many a demon in the past made vain attempts at trampling on our dream to be free and full.

Defying our emotions, great walls were erected to estrange us from ourselves.

Massive industrial military complexes were created to pulverize our august yearnings.

Some even went to the extent of crushing us with mighty tanks.

But none of their conspiracies availed. Instead, repugnant red robots of revolution relegated themselves to the object of regnant revulsion.

Buried beneath the ever swelling public obloquy, evil spirit of dialectic materialism ceased to cast its pernicious spell, and eventually committed suicide at the altar of glasnost and perestroika.

We emerged phoenix. Freedom triumphed, Liberty triumphed. We triumphed as a free spirit and an immortal Soul.

Fossilized skeletons of the innocent, victims of blood-mongering, will never cease to haunt potential fuhrers of human society.

Despots and tyrants of the world! Hearken to the caveat of Time. Your brutality and callousness cannot obliterate our ever blazing urge for freedom and liberty.

It is this immortal thirst that has defined our eternal existence.

Atrocious and ruthless, you are. Just like tiny moths, fascinated with the light of conflagration, you are destined to end up in ashes.

Your days are numbered.

Satyamewa jayate!

September, 2019

MOMENT OF MY SALVATION

O humanity,
How far is your destination?
How arduous is your journey?
Could you please accept me
As your trusted valet?
Pray have mercy upon me
It'll be the moment of my salvation

A SPLENDID MIX

O my Soul,
Each and every word
I write in your praise
Is the most beautiful poem

Each and every word
I pronounce in your glory
Is the most melodious music

Even a letter
Expressed in your reverence
Forms a splendid mix
Of arts and science,
And philosophy and religion

WE ARE A UNIQUE CREATURE

We are a unique creature
Both in terms of
Theory of Relativity, and
The Quantum Physics
We are as vast as the universe
We are as tiny as the tiniest
We are the source
Whence spring entire laws not Nature -
Known and unknown
The deeper we go into ourselves,
The more we get exposed to the mysteries of
       cosmos
Probably many more theories
Are yet to be revealed to surpass
Advait, Relativity and Quantum
Whatever might come
Will certainly be the echo of our Self
Because nothing does exist
Beyond Self

BEING HUMAN IS
NOT HEREDITARY

There are some
Who die but live forever
There are others
Who live but die forever
Life and death do not determine our fate
Rather we determine theirs
It is our own choice
Whether to live or to die
The ability to make it
Essentially makes us human
Being a human is not hereditary

I DON'T THINK THERE IS ANYTHING TO READ

I don't think
There is anything to read in books
Neither is there anything in scriptures
They are nothing but thick and dry barks of old
        trees -
Coarse, oafish, uneven, rude and arrogant
O my Soul,
How can I see the Nature of Reality
Through such inhospitable anomalies?
I don't think there are any books or scriptures
        except you
To see the ever ebullient face of Truth

LOVE

If used wisely
Can be a divine
Rendezvous
Where one can meet
One's own true being

If misused
Can be a deceptive
Contraption
Leading to ruin,
And destruction

I REALLY CELEBRATE

O Solitude,
I really celebrate
Your courtship with Silence,
The celestial fragrance
Of which
Has inspired
Countless seers and sages,
To dive deep
Into their own Being,
So they can fathom
The true
Nature of Reality,
And uncover the mystery
Behind existence

WHY AM I SO OBSESSED?

I don't know your shape and size
I don't know your color and creed
Neither do I know your race and religion
How inconceivable!
How inconspicuous!
How amorphous!
But still,
O my Soul,
Why am I so much obsessed with you?

I HAVE BEEN TRYING TO BECKON THE HISTORY

With enormous love and compassion
towards fellow beings in my heart,
I have been trying to beckon the History
for several millennia
Sometimes in the form of Time and Space
Both in the form of animate and inanimate entities,
        at other times
But the History,
perchance engrossed in its own course,
has failed to respond to my entreaty
However, I am not tired
Nor shall I ever be
I have a precious message to convey
Even more precious
than my own life, my journey and my destination
The divine message of 'universality of spirit'
Just like the dewdrops dripping from the petals
        of flowers,
once this message trickles down the shadow of
        History,
humanity will find its heart overwhelmed with
        poetic ambrosia

WHOM SHALL I ASK SAVE THEE?

O America,

Look how events are unfolding one after another

Some prone to encourage humans to realize their
full potential

Some most likely to decelerate the pace of
civilization, already achieved over thousands
of years

Again, some appearing to be nothing but red
herring, aimed at deflecting the attention of
Time

Really the world looks like a rainbow, with multiple
colors of human imagination

But who on earth can fathom its agony, arising
from its imminent evanescence?

Ambitions swirling as if they are going to devour
human species *en masse*

Vengeance and vendetta exploding as if it is going
to dehumanize entire mankind

Retribution flaring up as if it is going to incinerate
human existence

Where is the voice of sanity?

Why is it mum even in the face of our Being
standing on the edge of precipice?

O my Soul, whom shall I ask these questions save
thee?

A WOMAN TO ME

A woman to me
is a symbol of fascination
Not because of my attraction towards her
physiognomy
But because of solemn serenity, defining her Soul
She is not only the source of love and compassion
But also the perennial inspiration that even Mother
Nature always cherishes

UNITY IS OUR STRENGTH

O Bitterness,
O divisiveness,
O polarization,
O partisanship,
Why are you assaulting on our psyche?
Why are you attacking our institutions?
Why are you polluting our values?
Why are you bent on weakening us?
Why are you trying to undermine our voice?
Your sinister move cannot destroy our unity
Seemingly divided, polarized and partisan,
We are one, when it comes to strengthening our
        sovereign independence and integrity
We will ever remain united when it comes to
        defending our freedom, and that of fellow
        beings around the globe
No power on earth can shatter our unity
Just like Sun that seems divided in many pots of
        water, we are but one, regardless of visible
        disparities, and different hues
And this unity is our strength,
The sole source of our freedom and liberty

November 25, 2018

CONGRATULATIONS, MY DEAR CAPTAIN!

Janani janmabhoomishcha swargadapi gariyasi
VALMIKI RAMAYANA

O Captain, congratulations!

For your success in realizing the true Being of this great country and its brave people.

Except for the Founders, and a couple of others, barely had anyone truly realized the core of this great nation.

A new morning has dawned after the dark.

Far in the horizon has a nascent Sun emerged, with its all-embracing power, strength and compassion.

Exposed to a non-existent *deja vu*, Time seems convulsing.

Congratulations, my dear Captain!

Congratulations again and again!

We are so grateful that you have sailed us across the potentially disastrous and turbulent sea.

You have saved us from being mired in the morass of remorse and repentance.

You have rescued us from the devastating maelstrom of past aberrations.

You have again made us realize the true essence of being American.

You have enlightened us about the enormous strength and power, inherent in America and its great people.

I am fully aware of the unprecedentedly senseless attacks - both from within and without - showered upon your each and every well-intended moves.

How ludicrous and preposterous of them who are trying to invoke our sacred documents, while launching splenetic broadsides against your spectacular achievements!

However, our momentous strength and prosperity arising from your unswerving commitment to America and the American people has left detractors ashamed of themselves for their insidiousness.

O my dear Captain!

I am confident that you have enormous potential and extraordinary vision to add a new chapter in the annals of human civilization.

Under your iconoclastic leadership, the world is likely to undergo tectonic transformation.

The way you have been successful in rewriting the history of Korean Peninsula has made you truly a global leader, with impeccable leadership quality.

The destruction of ISIS, one of the most ruthless terrorist organizations ever seen in human history, has undoubtedly added a feather to your cap.

The repealing, revision and abrogation of 'unfair and horrible' treaties and agreements have not only restored our pride and prestige, but also helped bring the international order on an even keel.

O Captain, under your perspicacious leadership, America and its people have experienced exemplary economic boom and prosperity, sparsely seen before in the history of this country.

Your vision to create the United States Space Force will certainly add a new dimension to our definition of strength.

Your unvarnished love for our veterans and servicemen - whose sacrifice for the freedom and liberty of entire mankind on earth has made us eternally indebted to them - has served to steel ourselves against all potential odds.

Your disdain for political correctness, and an unyielding commitment to truth and justice have rendered corrupt elements, insidiously eating into the vitals of this Constitutional Republic, woefully naked and exposed.

Interestingly, your genuine search for justice, aimed at bolstering our sovereign independent existence as an exemplary beacon of order

and rule of law has left paranoid impostors
crying foul.

No doubt, the principle of check and balance
always demands that we rise above ideology-
hued technicalities, and listen to the voice
of our conscience, when it comes to feeling
poignant vibrations of our nation's heart.

O Captain, we are so proud that your leonine roar
from the vantage of America's unyielding
commitment to freedom and liberty has
compelled even redoubtable powerhouses of
contemporary world to rethink the course
they are currently pursuing.

In one way or another, they have brought
themselves to comply with your injunctions,
lest they should be cast aside by history.

This land of the brave is so grateful that:

Gone are the days when our highest office would
mock our national pride and prestige by
embarking on mission apology;

Gone are the days when we used to believe in the
absurd doctrine of 'leading from behind';

Gone are the days when we used to spurn the
'red line' set by ourselves, when it came to
destroying evil;

Gone are the days when we used to prostrate
before the brutal dictators and fanatical
mullahs, by heaping inordinate amount of

taxpayers' money on them, without anything
substantial in return;

Gone are the days when we used to be humiliated
and swindled by other countries;

Gone are the days when we used to be intimidated
by rogue states that would threaten us and
our closest allies with nuclear annihilation;

Gone are the days when we used to be treated as
nothing more than a feeble pushover by our
adversaries;

Gone are the days when we could do absolutely
nothing but watch as an inert and passive
onlooker the horrible beheading of our own
citizens, at the hands of most abhorrent
butchers of ISIS;

Gone are the days when our Chieftain used to
be snubbed ignominiously by authoritarian
forces around the world;

Gone are the days when, in apparent servitude, we
used to acquiesce in the diktats of so-called
allies who would enrich themselves at our
expense;

Gone are the days when elected leaders would
get ensnared in the sordid conspiracy of so-
called deep state, thereby jeopardizing our
democratic values and institutions;

Gone are the days when vile politicians would trade
our national security and national interests,
exclusively for their personal enrichment;

Gone are the days when corrupt and Machiavellian
political establishments could hold on to
power by keeping American people in
absolute dark;

Gone are the days when our national borders
could be breached by anyone with complete
impunity;

Gone are the days when extra-territorial criminal
elements could wreak havoc in our
communities, without eliciting any fitting
response;

Gone are the days when it was, more often than
not, believed that constitutions and laws are
meant to be broken, just like pie-crusts, to
borrow the famous saying of Jonathan Swift;

Gone are the days when 'hope' and 'change' had
turned into ludicrous misnomers, giving
way to despondence and stagnation;

Gone are the days when our national flag and
national anthem used to be derided as
something, insignificant and trivial.

O Captain, I am excruciatingly traumatized at the
way this country seems of late divided on the
basis of sex, gender, race, color and ideology.

Why can't political forces, media, and even
academia realize this evident corrosion?

Why do some of them seem further emboldened
to accelerate this degeneration, much to the

detriment of our national integrity, harmony and peace?

Why do they seem so impervious to brazen assaults on the part of alien elements on our sovereignty and independence?

Don't you think that some conspiratorial forces, both from within and without, might be trying to weaken this country, apparently with a view to nullifying our longstanding paramountcy in global politics?

And replace the present world order - based on liberal democracy and free market capitalist economy - with their authoritarian model that tends to thrive in the decimation of human conscience?

Honestly speaking, I am really nonplussed by media's exhilaration at inexplicable rendezvous with untruth, and Hollywood's transcendental tryst with morbid phantasies.

Equally mortified I am at our erudition and intellectuality being hijacked by fanatic vindictiveness and bigoted vendetta.

Even political establishments of both parties exude spasmodic symptoms of being swayed by some amorphous power's magic spell, when they consciously embark on inert inaction amid difficult situations warranting their prompt response and unwavering commitment.

Why have they failed to understand that their
    visceral antipathy towards each other could
    be the recipe for our adversaries to advance
    their macabre intent?
And the potential decline of this great country
    could easily translate into tyrannical forces
    overpowering the world, with freedom and
    liberty of mankind being the first victim of
    their demoniac disposition.
It seems as if our party establishments are in dire
    need of some highly sophisticated device
    attached to their ears, so they can hear the
    voice of their own conscience.
Freedom and democracy always demand that we
    elevate ourselves to a certain height and treat
    others the same way as we expect them to
    treat us.
However, I have no misgivings towards them,
    except the confidence that the day will come
    when they, too, will come to their senses.
And the ominous agenda of conspiracy, obstruction,
    hate and destruction will be thrown into
    oblivion.

O my Captain, I don't really care how the electoral
    politics plays out in future.
It is a slam dunk that your glorious legacy will
    never cease to rejuvenate and reinvigorate
    this great nation of the brave, with its ever-
    expanding vibrations, trying to encompass

entire human race with the most august
message of democracy, freedom and liberty.
And the reverential Star Spangled Banner will
evermore remain aloft with the exceptional
American spirit.

February, 2019

BLISS SUPREME

O my fellow beings,
Drink the nectar that I am
Enjoy the fragrance that I am
Come on, hurry up!
Have no hesitation
And dissolve yourself unto me
I am the bliss supreme

LET MY POEMS BE BURIED

My poems are the gospel of my Soul
Let them be buried in the slumber of Time
Let not the jingling of coins disturb their peace
Have patience, and just wait for the propitious
    moment
When they awake one day along with Time, entire
    world will start shuddering
Epochal volcanoes will erupt,
And tectonic plates will collide

I AM FULLY SATISFIED

I am fully
Satisfied with my life
I am proud of it
Unlike millions upon millions
I could make use of my life
To the best of my ability
Granted me by the Almighty
I believe
I have not at least wasted my life
Just in anticipation
Of Grim Reaper's ominous summons
I do confess sincerely
I might have, wittingly or unwittingly,
Committed some infractions
But, O my Soul,
They must have been offset
By my unalloyed devotion
To your sovereignty

HOW VACUOUS!

A callous giant,
With hundreds of millions crushed
Under its monolithic boots,
Dreaming of devouring the world;
How ominous!

A vindictive bear,
With human blood on its mouth and claws,
Contemplating the restoration
Of its ancestral tyranny;
How portentous!

Pampered by evil spirits,
A wayward pipsqueak
Threatening the mighty symbol of freedom
With nuclear annihilation;
How ludicrous!

Bushy *Raktabeejas*,
With recourse to violence and terror,
Seeking to plunge human civilization
Into qayamat of darkness;
How obnoxious!

Oblivious indeed to
The Nature of Reality,
They all seem intent on
Decimating Truth;
How vacuous!

May, 2019

DEFINITION OF
A HUMAN

Behind the ugliness of imperfection
is hidden the beauty of perfection
Behind the cacophony of hubbub
is hidden the melody of silence
Behind the shadow of darkness
is hidden the brightness of light
And this is what defines a human

I WANT TO EMPTY MYSELF

I want to empty myself

I want to shed all my acquisition, desire, ambition,
and even relations before I depart

I don't want my journey to the other shore
encumbered by worn-out baggages

Above everything else, I want to get rid of entire
attachments - ever insidious and corrosive

I want to travel light

I don't even want to carry with me anything that I
owe my Creator

Indebtedness, whether it be to the Creator or to
some corporeal entity, is always burdensome

It might jeopardize the bliss, oozing out emptiness

LET'S FATHOM IT

Life is a penance
Let's perform it
A play of divinity
Let's propitiate it
An eternal beauty
Let's appreciate it
An urge for freedom
Let's fathom it

ETERNALLY FIXATED

O my Soul,
How solemn your gait is!
And how sublime your panache!
How soothing your poise is!
And how inspiring your persona!
I am eternally fixated on you
Just like Sphinx on the moon

AS I GROW OLD

As I grow old I feel as if I am
about to be integrated
into the vast and unfathomable
realm of Spirit, spread across
the entire creation of God
It gives me exhilaration,
beyond imagination

HOW ARDUOUS
THIS JOURNEY IS!

O my Soul,
I know how arduous this journey is
It might take even millions of years
But I won't stop until
I get immersed
In your divine resplendence
I won't hesitate
Even to traverse the vast Spacetime
Neither do I get scared of
Diving into the subatomic universe
Of neutron, proton, electron, photon and quarks
O my Soul,
I won't even take rest
Until I find myself
Both in your immanence
And transcendence
After all,
My journey is an undying quest
For my own definition

O ANIMUS!

O animus,
Don't you try to overpower me
Never shall you find me
Submit to your dark spell
Don't you ever expect me to turn into Cain
Whose hands are stained with blood
Of his own brother, Abel

O DEMOCRACY, O RULE OF LAW!

O Democracy,

O Rule of Law,

Are you going to incarcerate us?

Are you going to incinerate us?

Are you going to devour us?

Why are you serving as a convenient cloak for the knavery of knaves?

And treason of the traitors?

Why do you pave their way for the betrayal of this nation?

Why do you inspire such elements to toy with the security of our beloved motherland?

Why are you conniving at their insouciance about the safety of our countrymen?

Why are you allowing them to play the ominous cards of race, religion, color and gender?

Do you think their conscience is waging a mutiny or they are just playing a cat's-paw?

Don't you see their effrontery of putting their ambition ahead of America and the Americans?

Do you think that their lust for power is more important than the future of this nation and its people?

Is Democracy mere a vehicle to elevate oneself to the position of power?

Is Rule of Law nothing more than a tool to destroy one's political opponents?

O Democracy, O Rule of Law,
I know love for the country and commitment to certain values can only make you active and vibrant
Their absence among politicos tends to render you completely effete, paralyzed and disoriented
But even having been aware of this, O Democracy, O Rule of Law, where shall I go to lodge a complaint?
To me, there seems certainly something going amiss
What good is Democracy if it cannot bring all forces together, when it comes to bolstering national sovereignty and independence?
What good is Rule of Law if it fails to inspire all forces to join hands, when it comes to buttressing honor and dignity of citizenry?
What good are these values if they cannot strengthen the integration and unity of our Constitutional Republic?

O Democracy, O Rule of Law,
It is really sad that under your watch, our values seem corroding, and institutions crumbling
And the powermongers are happy to further precipitate this decadence
Can't you hear the groan of this nation?

Can't you feel the excruciating pain this nation is
    going through?

O Democracy, O Rule of Law
Conspiracy cannot be your trait
Vendetta and vengeance cannot be your character
Hatred and smear cannot be your signature
Corruption and misuse of authority cannot be
    your imprint
If you don't even have qualm about condoning
    such unscrupulousness, what is the
    difference between your realm and that of
    brutal dictators from countries like Russia,
    China, North Korea, Venezuela, Syria, Iran
    and the likes?
Isn't it that the sole purpose of those dictators
    is to concentrate entire state authority in
    themselves, no matter how stained their
    hands are with blood of the innocent?
Certainly there is a vast difference between your
    solemn tranquility and sanguinary bedlam
    of those regimes
And, of course, there must be!

April, 2019

HOW TRAUMATIZING IT IS!

O America,
I can totally understand your predicaments,
I can feel your pain,
I know how agonizing it is
To be betrayed by our own offspring
How traumatizing it is:
When our own children stab in the back
When our own children conspire against us
When our own children collaborate with enemies
    to undermine us
When our own children incite enemies to mount
    assaults on us
When our own children jeopardize our honor and
    dignity
When our own children smear us only to please
    our adversaries
When our own children incite enemies to encroach
    on our lands
When our own children inspire aliens to plunder
    our wealth and prosperity
When our own children are bent on reducing us
    to a non-entity
When our own children emerge as our existential
    threat

April, 2019

YOU ARE THE IMMORTAL PHILOSOPHY

Who is not infatuated with your grandeur?
Who is not fascinated with your majesty?
Who is not smitten with your panache?
Who is not enchanted by your graciousness?
O America,
You are a superb imagination of the Being Supreme.
You are the intrinsic urge of the Soul divine.
You are the greatest philosophy ever conceived.
The immortal philosophy of freedom and liberty.

I KNOW

I know
My poems are not anybody's concern
Not even mine
It they are anyone's
It is my Soul's

LOVE AND AMOUR

Ensconced in the amorous embrace of Solitude,
Silence once sighed in coquetry, "I wish to
be eternally embedded in you, just like light
in the moon."

His cup of love apparently brimming with amatory
passion, Solitude gently tightened his grasp
and let himself be immersed in her empyrean
realm.

Solitude and Silence, since time immemorial,
have been sharing with entire living beings
the soothing fragrance of their divine
communion.

Even mountains and valleys, plains and prairies,
and deserts and plateaus seem desperate to
savor the celestial perfume.

O UNTRUTH!

O untruth!
Why do you render yourself so low?
Why can't you feel your own decadence?
Why are you so desperate to destroy yourself?
If you still want to plunge really low,
Mariana Trench might be happy to play a host
But I beg you not to keep holding on to our Fourth
        Estate
before you make a suicidal dive

November, 2018

POTENTIAL EMERGENCE OF A SAVAGE BEAST

Democracy (D) and US Constitution (USC) in this country have ever remained bosom friends for more than two hundred years, since the independence of America in 1776.

Cordial sharing of weal and woes between the two friends has always made their relationship vibrant, exemplary and inspiring.

D was once stunned to hear the ululation of USC who seemed uncontrollably shaken by the striking of some potential catastrophe.

"What is it that has made you so perturbed?" with a brimming cup of empathy, D solemnly said to his dearest friend. "Is there anything that I can do to resolve your quandary?"

USC, in a trembling voice, tinged with plaintive supplication, said, " With an abiding faith in my dispensation, people of this land had chosen their representatives to form the Legislative Branch that was supposed to act in cooperation with other two branches of government, executive and judiciary."

"What can be most unfortunate than this," lamented USC. "As if swayed by the black magic of some evil forces, most of them seem to have been metamorphosed into snakes and serpents, and have started spewing venom?"

Superbly idealistic as he was, USC had expected all members of that institution to focus themselves on how to establish the 'Kingdom of God' on earth, and to enact laws accordingly, apparently in tune with the spirit of US Declaration of Independence. Extremely frustrated at the way the Congress had consciously stigmatized the basic philosophy, underlying the principle of check and balance, USC bemoaned, "Even judicial processes have not remained unscathed by their aberrance."

To him, Congress, in which people of this country had pinned a great hope, appeared to have been reduced to an assemblage of senseless reptiles, prone to apathy and inertia on the one hand, and hatred and vindictiveness, smear and insinuation on the other.

He was profoundly mortified at the way people seemed inclined to weigh allegedly lackadaisical performance of his dearest friend, D, against seemingly spectacular achievements of Evils, that have long been thriving on the decimation of human conscience.

The absurd proposition being floated by some rabid reptiles - that we need to follow in the footsteps of discredited Evils - coupled with the emerging proxy voice of eschatological fanaticism would make him feel as if cruel destiny was piercing his heart with a burning arrow.

A large section of so-called fourth estate's obsequiousness to the ominous deviance of politics had left him no less dismayed.

"If they can't restore themselves to their original condition, and are subjected to the same fate as Gregor Samsa, entire world might once again plunge into unimaginable apocalypse," he lamented.

Convinced that almost each and every act of the US Congress would, in one way or another, have a profound impact across the world, USC could hardly countenance its deviation.

"If those snakes and serpents persist in their macabre pursuits, defying the sacred *Laxman rekha* set by you, not only the people of this land, but entire mankind will be forced to suffer untold devastation on earth," said USC. "It is most likely that from the sea of men will emerge a giant monster who will instantly decimate you and me, as a prelude to the establishment of a diabolic regime, based on blood and terror."

He also warned that the demonic monster would then start devouring tens of millions of people around the world, in the same way a blue whale swallows from the large shoal of krill in the deep ocean.

Although intrinsically appalled at the apocalyptic prognostication of USC, D, with a veneer of imperturbability, wondered in his dulcet tone, "My dear friend, why are you so pessimistic about the future of this country and mankind; are you really serious about what you are prophesying?"

USC, as he was omniscient, started chronicling the events of the past, and prudently concluded that massive perversion on the part of megalomaniac politicos, with fanatical support of masses' warped dispositions, ironically emanating from the exercise of absolute freedom, sometimes gives birth to an unimaginably savage beast in human society.

"Who can predict the future," said USC with a tearful sigh. "But I am really scared that these snakes and serpents might one day lead us to crucifixion, along with our most beloved offspring - freedom and liberty."

Suddenly D found himself awakened by the
euphonic sound of conch shell, coming from
a nearby temple.

The eerie ordeal he had gone through just a few
moments ago rendered him completely
nonplussed. Once he pondered over the cause,
he found that he had by mistake ingested
some kind of hallucinogen, presumably
supplied by conspiratorial alien spies.

May, 2019

MY DEEPEST OBEISANCE

An infinitesimally tiny dot
Seemingly lost somewhere
In the vastness of universe
Fervently seeking to identify itself
With the eternal and infinite power
Responsible for creating the cosmos!
O human,
I am proud of your wondrous spirit!
I am proud of your pious existence!
Unto thee, my deepest obeisance!

MY POEMS

My poems are not mere words and phrases
Neither are they vapid and vacuous sentences
They are the vibration of my Soul
Since my Soul is immortal,
They, too, will never die
Infinite is my Soul
So are my poems
They are the eternal melody,
With dazzling effulgence of divinity
Like my Soul,
They are the definition
Of both beginning and the end
In them is embedded
The history of creation,
Sustenance and dissolution
They are as much the echo of the distant past
As they are the signature of present
Future finds itself ensconced in their embryo

JUST STOP THIS NONSENSE

Let me speak
Let me express myself
Let me speak my mind
Pray don't stop me from speaking
Pray don't stop me from expressing myself
Pray don't stop me from speaking my mind
Let me speak the history
Let me speak the past
Let me speak the reality
Try to understand my speech in its right context
Don't try to misinterpret it
Don't try to distort it out of context
History is history, you cannot erase it
Even today scientists can hear the echo of Big Bang
Supposedly an incident 13 plus billion years old
Just because I speak, it doesn't necessarily mean
    that I align myself with past wrong doings,
    potentially associated with my words
I just want to shed light on some issues that deeply
    concern humans and humanity
If you think that even pronouncing certain words
    and phrases is so execrable, and therefore
    must be banned
I dare you to burn all the dictionaries and books
    of history

Because they will never allow those execrables
        to die
You will find yourself being evermore mocked by
        their obstinacy
In fact, your perverted interpretation and devious
        manipulation, rather than those words and
        phrases, are depraved and despicable
It is nothing but a sinister attempt at muzzling me
An ominous foray into my freedom of speech and
        expression
A brazen trampling of my First Amendment Rights
Therefore, just stop this nonsense

O FREEDOM!

O freedom!

Spread your wings across the globe

Let everyone realize your tranquil serenity

Let each corner of this earth resound with your
sweet melody

And let the ambience of this world be perfumed
with your eternal fragrance

O freedom!

Pray invite everyone to get dissolved into your
joyful realm

O MOUNTAINS!

O mountains, oceans, deserts, prairies, plains,
    plateaus,
O sky and the earth,
O space and your sprawling paraphernalia,
I feel so privileged to have you all in my Self
I feel so honored to have you all in my Being
I know I will not cease to be as long as you are
You will not cease to be as long as I am
We are all part of the fullness that never ceases to
    be full
We are all full in our own respects
Naturally, our conglomeration is full, too
We all share same attributes - eternity, immanence,
    imperishability and infinity
We might change our shape, size, symmetry and
    proportion to suit the longing of our own Self
But the core of all of us will always remain the same
We are the Self Supreme unto ourselves!

I REPRESENT THE AGE

O America, I represent the age.

Like every human, I am the child of my age, no doubt.

Yet I can see far beyond its boundary.

As a free spirit, I have been able to transcend the emotions, impulses, prejudices, proclivities and dispositions of the age.

I don't find myself constrained in any kind of straitjackets.

My vision cannot be stymied by the maneuverings of Time and Space.

Neither my judgment can be darkened by the material modes of Nature.

I am an enigmatic journey the destination of which can never be fully fathomed.

In my transcendental persona are embedded both profundity and immanence of divinity.

I am so subtle that even subtlety envies.

I reside in the heart of every human, and identify myself with their undying urge for freedom.

The fire within me is not likely to die down.

With the passage of time it seems to have further increased.

I don't think it will extinguish even after my death.

Most probably, my demise might turn it into an apocalyptic inferno.

Because the world is in a frantic search for some
tectonic transformation.
Entire values, institutions, customs, traditions and
even our socio-cultural mores are in dire
need of timely mutation.
Were it not for the Supernova, Homo sapiens would
not have come into existence.

YOUR VICTORY IS PREORDAINED

America,
Protect your borders
Protect your sovereignty
Protect your independence
The world of politics is utterly vile
Insouciance will further increase your vulnerability
Naivety will further deepen your woes
There are forces out there who want to destroy
    your Soul
Freedom and liberty of mankind has never been
    imperiled
Were it not for you, freedom would have already
    been decapitated, and liberty devoured
Humanity would have been thrown into the dark
    dungeon of dystrophy
America, stand as a mighty mountain against
    violent storms
Serve as an oasis for embattled humans and
    humanity
Assaulted as they are from all directions
Make no delay in defeating all kinds of profane
    proclivities
Rise against the dirge of depraved disposition
And destroy the entire inimical impulses, bent on
    depriving you of your own Soul

They are nothing but the bestial outburst of
Kauravas' *folie de grandeur*
You are endowed with the exceptional power and
strength of the Pandavas
Lord's blessing in the form of Truth, Justice and
Righteousness is always with you
Your victory is preordained

January, 2019

RISE UP, LOOK!

"O Americans,
My dearest offspring,
Are you still sleeping and taking your rest?
It is enough!
The hour has come.
Look, the paragon of freedom and liberty is likely
        to be betrayed into the hands of enemies.
Rise up, look!
They who betray me are at hand."
I have absolutely no idea
why this poignant cry of our beloved motherland
is constantly ricocheting,
off the corners of my heart!

April, 2019

SPRING IS APHRODISIAC

Spring is aphrodisiac

Intoxicated by the flirtation of nubile flowers, hummingbirds suck nectar from their lustful lips

Dancing to the tune of budding amour within themselves, bumblebees try to attract flowers' prurient glances

Wafting ecstatically in the air, butterflies commingle themselves as if to remind mortals of the divine union between Purusha and Prakriti

Ravished by the amorous perfume, pervading the ambience of Spring, unruly senses start courting coy emotions

Spring is aphrodisiac

WHEN I CLOSE MY EYES

When I open my eyes
I don't see anything
When I close my eyes
I see everything
How paradoxical my vision is!
How enigmatic my transport is!
When I walk the earth, it always reminds me:
Soil is the response to my hubris
Soil is the response to my chutzpah
When I look up the sky, it always inspires me:
Infinity I am
Eternity I am
Sandwiched between the stalactite of the sky and
          stalagmite of the earth
I always wonder who I am, and who it is that carves
          out my destiny

AMERICA, THOU SHALT …

America,

Thou shalt not give in to 'serpents'

Thou shalt not be cowered by the 'generation of
vipers'

Thou shalt not be intimidated by 'pharisees'

And thou shalt not fear 'scribes'

Thou shalt protect thyself and thy offspring

Thou shalt not compromise thy fundamental
principles

Thou shalt not allow thy ideals to be destroyed

Thou shalt not tolerate the infringement of thy
persona

Thou shalt never cease to be the custodian of
freedom and liberty

Thou shalt be the savior of mankind

Thou shalt obliterate tyranny and despotism from
earth

Thou shalt be the symbol of truth and righteousness

Thou shalt be the leader of the free world

Thou shalt forever uphold the doctrine of
Universality of Spirit

Thou shalt not be content with the Kingdom of
God on earth

Thou shalt create the Empire of Truth both on
earth and space

April, 2019

WHO AM I TO JUDGE?

Who am I to judge my own life
Whether I lived it to the fullest?
It is Time that wields the sole authority to make
the evaluation
Even for Time, I know, it takes long to pass
judgment,
Let alone the world, contemporaneous with me
Human assessment invariably tends to be flawed
and fraught
I believe, Time's judgment will be based on the
conflation of both subjective reflexes and
objective reality
Time always plays a free and impartial judiciary,
Transcendental to human emotions and impulses

ULTIMATE PRAYER OF MY LIFE

O my Soul,
You are my world
You are my universe
You are my journey
You are my destination
Nothing can I conceive beyond you
You are the temple
where I pay homage to the Supreme Being
You are the church
where I recite 'sermon on the mount'
You are the mosque
where I kneel before the Merciful One
You are the monastery
where I meditate on nirvana
You are the solemn rendezvous
where I commiserate with your creation
O my Soul,
The esoteric harmony between science and
        spirituality,
Let me take thousands of births
only to serve and salute your creation
And this is the ultimate prayer of my life

O UNKNOWN ENTITY!

O unknown entity,
hidden behind my existence,
Who are you, and what do you want of me?
Do you want me to dance to your tune?
Or you want me to pursue my own free will?
It has been an eternal confusion
that I always want to be clear about

WHAT COULD BE ...?

What could be more ecstatic than to be lost in the solitude of one's own being?

What could be more romantic than the courtship between silence and solitude?

Why can't we dive deep into silence, so we can converse with our true being?

Why do we, in spite of ourselves, tend to veer into the dark of illusion?

Were it not for my tears, what could have cleansed the agony of human destiny?

"YOURS IS THE BODY, YOU'RE SELF"

Unable to tolerate my suffering, Agony once said to me, "You boast of having multitude of relatives, friends and well-wishers, but I don't see even your beloved wife and children come forward to share what you have been going through."

He went on to add, "I don't think their words of love and sympathy, however sincere and earnest, can relieve you of torture you have been subjected to."

On the one hand I couldn't help appreciating his remarks because of their empathetic overtone. But I was not happy with his comments about my wife and children, on the other.

"Your sympathy is nothing but crocodile's tears," I said to him, as if incensed at his insinuation. "You know it very well that you are the very source of my pain."

"Don't try to misunderstand me," with a streak of solicitude in his smiling face, Agony responded. "I have never harbored any intention of hurting you, neither shall I do so anytime in future."

"If not you, then who is it that always tortures me, with complete disregard for my innocence and inculpability?" I blurted out.

"It is solely your nescience that hoodwinks you into identifying your Self with your body, which is amenable to the onslaughts of natural forces," said Agony, in a solemn voice. "And therefore, your nescience is responsible for your suffering, not me."

Befuddled by his abstruse argument, I begged him to clarify the distinction between my Self and my body.

"Yours is the body, you're Self," revealed Agony.

I don't know how long it will take for humans to fathom the truth, underlying Agony's mystical statement.

"CERTAINLY YOU CAN, IF YOU WISH"

One day I asked my Self, "Who am I."

He said, "You are me."

I asked him, "What is your real identity then?"

He said, "I am the Supreme Being."

I asked, "Why do you call yourself the Supreme Being?"

He said, "Because I am the creator, sustainer and destroyer of the universe, and nothing in this universe can even move without my will."

I asked, "If I am you, and you are so powerful, why can't I even transcend my tiny body?"

He said, "Certainly you can, if you wish."

O AMERICANS, REALIZE THE AMERICA

My dear fellow Americans,
Realize the America, hidden somewhere in your
heart
He is without name and form
He is in your body and mind
He is in the elements that you are made of
He is in your senses, ego and intellect
Yet He is transcendent to these all
He is the sole power that energizes the universe
He is the sole authority that maintains order in the
cosmos
He is the sole guardian whence sprouts entire
evolution
There is nothing that He does not perform
Yet He is the one who never acts
O Americans,
Try to find Him in your heart
Try to see Him in your Self
Try to fathom Him in your consciousness
He alone is the absolute reality -
All pervasive, eternal and infinite
Chant every moment -
America,
Tattwamasi, tattwamasi, tattwamasi!

June, 2019

I MIGHT GET LOST!

O my Soul,
Where shall I seek you,
In the mesmerizing beauty
Of this phenomenal world,
Or in unity,
Underlying the apparent world
Of dazzling colors, and
Lustrous multiplicity?

Perhaps you don't know
How thirsty I am
For your graceful audience!

Over millions of years
Of undying yearning
For your divine *sakshatkar*,
I don't know
When I morphed myself
Into undulating waves, and
Dancing particles,
Adorning the vast ocean of Spacetime

O my Soul,
I am afraid I might get lost
In the eternal enigma,
Surrounding
The Nature of Reality,
Before even getting a glimpse
Of your shadow!

OMINOUS INCUBUS

I don't know why I feel like pouring myself out
even at the slightest provocation of an
amorous smile, streaking the scarlet lips of
a rose.

Sometimes I feel like playing apoplectic thunder
when my passion, emotion and desires get
bruised at the hands of some nemesis.

Many a time it has occurred to me that I can hardly
resist the temptation of owning the fruits of
someone's sweat and toil.

There is no denying that having been consumed
by *Dhritarashtrian* impulses, I might have
suffered from clouded discernment and
impaired judgment.

When I view surroundings from the perspective
of my status, position and accomplishments,
I feel like looking down on fellow beings, as
nothing more than insignificant worms and
insects.

Any kind of acquisitions even on the part of my
own relatives gives me enormous strain
and stress that I can hardly do away with,
without lampooning their person.

No wonder,
This is how we, as ordinary human beings, get
swayed by Nature's deceitful maneuverings.

Perhaps saints, sages and seers are right when
they suggest that only the true knowledge
about the Nature of Reality can remove this
ominous incubus, hovering over our destiny.

I AM BUT A CLEAR MIRROR

You are bigoted
You accuse me of bigotry
You are fanatic
You accuse me of fanaticism
You are racist
You accuse me of racism
You are xenophobic
You accuse me of xenophobia
You are radical
You accuse me of radicalism
You are extremist
You accuse me of extremism
You are misogynist
You accuse me of misogyny
Please try to understand
I am but a clear mirror
That does not reflect itself
Rather what you see in it
Is your own reflection

June, 2019

CHART YOUR OWN COURSE

O youths of the world,
Why are you behaving as if you were an old
mountain - despondent and neurasthenic?
A mute spectator to the devastating havocs, wreaked
by deviant tornadoes and hurricanes
Why do you look so inert, complacent and resigned?
Why can't you feel within yourself the simmering
volcano, determined to swallow the tyrants
and despots of earth?
Why can't you feel within yourself the swirling
inferno, intent on devouring the enemies of
human civilization?
Why can't you realize that you aren't merely an
unconscious mass of blood, flesh and bones?

Just take a moment, peer into your own Self
You are an indomitable spirit, with enormous
power and strength
Servitude and subservience is alien to your nature
You are the true architect of your own destiny
Freedom and liberty is your inalienable right, and
prosperity your prerogative
You have every right to dismantle the walls
that stand in the way to your legitimate
aspirations

You were the ones who had destroyed the despotic
anachronistic order by storming the Bastille
You were the ones who had challenged the mighty
Evil Empire by dismantling Berlin Wall
You were the ones who had, with exceptional
courage and boldness, dared defy the brutal
totalitarian Dragon, standing against their
mighty tanks
You were the ones who had forced the oppressive
regimes across the Middle East to get down
on their knees
Wherever there is political freedom and economic
prosperity in this world, that is nothing but
the true definition of your inherent power
and strength

Therefore, O youths of the world,
Arise and awake!
Look at the Pandavas
How they destroyed Bhishma, Drona,
Karna, Duryodhana and the likes - evil
manifestations of untruth and injustice
Why can't you realize that even your world
today is fraught with evil forces' devilish
machinations

O youths of the world,
Never give in to the illusion that you are alone

Once you commit yourself to the cause of freedom,
 your faith and conviction, courage and
 fortitude will never cease to accompany you
Therefore, O youths of the world,
Arise and awake with redoubled spirit and iron
 determination of Arjuna
Make no delay in facing off evil forces *en masse*

If there is any religion that inhumes your Self, just
 incinerate it
If there is any political system that tramples on
 your Self, just obliterate it
If there is any faith that demeans your Self, just
 decimate it

O youths of the world,
Don't ever get entangled in trifles that tend to
 enervate your Self
Rise above senseless bickering, relating to race,
 religion, color, ethnicity, gender and origin
Each human, as a divine Soul, is great in himself
No one is superior, neither is anyone inferior
The delusion of supremacy is equally abominable
No matter, whether it be white or black, red or brown
Rise yourself, and inspire your fellow beings to arise
Together you can change the world
And illuminate the destiny of entire mankind
Don't ever get enmeshed in bigotry, fanaticism and
 superstition

Neither any religion nor any creed nor faith is
    above you
As a pure, pristine, eternal and infinite Self, you
    are above them all
You are divine unto yourself
If you have to worship any God, worship your
    fellow beings
If you have to prostrate before any God, prostrate
    before your fellow beings
If you have to propitiate any God, propitiate your
    fellow beings
Because they are none other than you
The same manifestation of divinity
And the same God as you are

Do't get swayed by the wizardly spell of so-called
    religious preachers who have nothing to
    preach except superstition, hate, fanaticism,
    bigotry and extremism
They invest their entire energy to create Scriptures
    and Gods out of nothing
They use their specious imagination to reinforce
    apocryphal accounts and false narratives
They exploit your gullibility for perpetuating
    a dark regime, obviously hellbent on
    destroying your faith in your own pure Self
They always strive to nurture their demonic order
    by making you feel as if you are nothing but
    a tiny speck of blood, flesh and bones

Even more pernicious are the forces that try to
    transmogrify your Self into a pliant part
    of their gigantic machine, and subject your
    existence to eternal incarceration
Don't ever get mesmerized by nectarine
    pronouncements of such devious elements
    that always conspire to strip you of your
    inalienable right to freedom and prosperity
Try to recognize the immense power within your
    Self
And chart your own course to freedom, liberty
    and prosperity

April, 2019

WHAT RITUAL DO I NEED TO PERFORM?

O my Soul,
How long shall I have to wait
To get a glimpse of your beauty?

Which path do I need to pursue
To see the footprints of your love?

Where shall I have to travel
To see the dance of your shadow?

When shall I start hearing
The enchanting music of your divinity?

What ritual do I need to perform
To be blessed with your grace?

A RELENTLESS YAJNA

My dear fellow beings,
As an indigent myself,
Living a spartan life
I can't give you gold and diamond,
Wealth and prosperity
But I will certainly give you something,
Far more important and precious
Than the entire wealth of this world -
A new awakening of life, and an escape from death
My life is an unceasing mission,
Aimed at making you realize your true Being
A relentless *yajna*, in the truest sense of the term

I DARE YOU

O science,
I dare you to explore a new realm
Where humans can enjoy the bliss supreme,
Without denying senses their legitimate aspirations

I WON'T RETURN WITHOUT REPAYING

O Almighty,
Pray rest assured
I won't return
Without repaying the debt
I owe you

Omniscient you are
I need not explain
How I am tailoring my mind,
Body and senses
To suit your longings
How I am honing
My intellect and ego
To accord with your injunctions

O Almighty,
My life is a mission
Dedicated to your beloved creation
Since I can't see you anywhere
Except in their Self
I do relentlessly celebrate
The doctrine of Self
Since I can't see you anywhere
Except in fellow beings
I tirelessly sing
The Universality of Spirit

O Almighty,
What makes me truly exulted
Is the echo of this gospel
That I can hear
In treatises of philosophers,
From Plato and Kant
To Hegel and Nietzsche
In discoveries of scientists
From Darwin and Einstein
To Niels Bohr and Hawking

It gives me utmost pleasure
Even to ponder that
This is the only gospel
That can travel across
Time and Space
And this is the only absolute
That can traverse both
Science and spirituality

O Almighty,
Pray allow me to take my devotion
To this gospel of yours
As the repayment of debt
I owe you

I CAN'T DESCRIBE
IN WORDS

O America,
I can't describe in words the excruciating pain I am
　　going through
Maybe, it might be one of the most formidable
　　ordeals presented by our destiny
We are absolutely devoid of any options, but to
　　accept it as the worst nightmare
The cruel politics of deception, dissimulation and
　　dissolution is eating into your vitals
Democratic institutions are undergoing
　　unprecedented strain
Congress has been used as the launching pad of
　　lethal projectiles against political opponents
It seems to have ceased to be a forum to discuss
　　and debate policies, programs and principles
The *raison d'être* of this institution seems to be
　　interred into the grave of insatiable vengeance
　　and hatred
It is no more an institution, serving comprehensive
　　interests of our nation and 'We the People'
It has been turned into an unceremonious podium
　　to spew venom
Some have even gone to the extent of unabashedly
　　turning it into a platform, meant for bolstering
　　evil designs of our declared enemies

How dare they betray the trust of American people,
   by jeopardizing the basic foundations of this
   constitutional republic?
How dare they deflect our entire attention from
   ominous realities and macabre threats, prone
   to dismantle our position as the leader of
   Free World?
And get the entire nation hooked unto red herrings,
   in the form of voodoo fantasies and hoodoo
   delusions?
Enemies of democracy, freedom and liberty
   around the world are striding by leaps and
   bounds, while we have been forced into the
   disastrous vortex of Shakuni politics

Why can't our so-called representatives find a
   bipartisan solution to the immigration crisis
   that is steadily leading us to dystopia?
Why can't they concentrate themselves on seeking
   solution to multiple threats, emanating from
   totalitarian dictators and rogue regimes?
Why can't they focus themselves on finding ways
   and means to perpetuate our predominance
   in global politics, as an ardent advocate of
   democracy, freedom and liberty?
Why can't they involve themselves in the
   formulation of policies and programs that
   help America and the Americans remain
   as the greatest civilization, ever created by
   humans on earth?

O congressmen,
I don't think great people of this country want you
        to be ever obsessed with sleazy contempt
        and vulgar scorn
They might gratify your warped impulses, but
        they can't serve the basic interests of America
        and the American people
Neither can they nurture and nourish the
        fundamental values and principles, this
        constitutional republic has always stood for

O congressmen,
I have nothing but pity on you!
Woe to you, who use that sacred institution for
        advancing petty personal interests
Woe to you, who use that sacred institution for
        enriching yourself at the cost of America and
        the Americans
Woe to you, who use that sacred institution for
        settling a score on personal enemies
Woe to you, who use that sacred institution for
        getting involved in corruption and abuse of
        power
Woe to you, who have not only betrayed the trust
        of innocent Americans, but also worked to
        undermine democracy, freedom and liberty,
        bequeathed from extraordinary genius and
        enormous sacrifice of our Founders
Woe to you, who, just having been elected as
        representatives, consider yourselves above

laws and Constitution, and treat people as
nothing more than benighted serfs

O congressmen,
I don't have even a scintilla of prejudice or enmity
towards you, your organization, and your
commitment, if there is any, to American
people and this great nation
What has inspired me to embark on this seeming
pontification is my undying loyalty to
America and its brave people who have
always stood for democracy, freedom and
liberty, not only for themselves, but for entire
mankind
As a bard of the present, it is also no less incumbent
upon me to get our political landscapes
recorded for future generations
O congressmen,
I will still be looking forward to the day when I can
declare from the public podium: "I am really
proud of you."

April, 2019

COMMITMENT TO MANKIND

What is Universality of Spirit,
What is Universality of Soul,
If not an abiding commitment
To mankind as a whole?

HOW FORTUNATE I AM!

O my Soul,
Sometimes life plays an agony
I can't even describe how unbearable it is
It does traumatize me to the core of my Being
I feel as if I were a dry and wizened leaf,
About to fall from the tree
My hairs stand on their end
My mouth gets parched
I do experience perceptible trembling,
Prone to break my will
I can see nothing except the dark
The world before me starts crumbling

O my Soul,
How fortunate I am!
Even in such an excruciating moment,
I can rescue myself
As soon as I take refuge in you
Again I start experiencing the beauty of life and
    this world
My will, vigor, and strength get exceptionally soared
I get more focused on my pursuit than even before
My vision becomes clear
Finally I find myself established in my own Self

O my Soul,
Were it not for your mercy
I would have been totally devastated long ago

I know it is your grace and mercy towards me
That you want me to go through such horrendous
          an ordeal every once in a while
So I can withstand any onslaughts of destiny
No matter how formidable it is
After all, I have your mission to accomplish

I OFTEN FEEL MESMERIZED

O Supreme Consciousness,
I feel exhilarated
When I find
Scientific and philosophical giants
Wading in the inexplicable
Enigma of your splendor

O Universal Consciousness,
How esoteric and enchanting you are!
You are the sole vibration of the vast cosmos
The mystery of the nanoscopic world you are
There is nothing in the cosmos
In which you are not immanent
Yet you are detached and transcendent
Neither science nor philosophy
Can map the magic of your enigma

O Universal Being,
How wondrous you are!
Even scientific giants of mortal world
Find themselves caught off guard
When you play a mediator
Between seemingly two opposite poles,
Science and spirituality

I often feel mesmerized
When I spy the panorama
Of your divine *lila*
Through the enlightened window
Of my own Soul!

I AM NOTHING ...

In the tiniest
Of the tiny is hidden
The power Supreme

Will death someday
Become a story
Of the past?

Ecstasy bursts
Out of union with
One's own Self

I am nothing
Therefore
I'm everything

In the silence of
Nature hides the
Mystery of creation

Everything
That seems real
Is but an illusion

I am lost
In the journey
Towards myself

How can you define me
Mere in terms of proton,
Neutron and electron?

Flower of life
Smiles with the
Fragrance of love

Our conscience
Is the echo of
Nature of Reality

The world of void
Is brimming with
Music of fullness

Deep within your
Self lurks potential
For greatness

A vast universe
Is hidden in the heart
Of a tiny atom

From fragrance
Of flowers exudes
Romance of Nature

In silence of
Solitude I hear
Music of Soul

WHO CAN BUT ...?

Who can but
Solitude fathom the
Depth of silence?

Who can but
Solitude know the
Secret of silence?

Who can but
Solitude adore the
Beauty of silence?

Who can but
Solitude hear the
Music of silence?

Who can
But solitude
Court silence?

SOME SURREAL SPARKS

Those who speak with their eyes do not reveal the truth. Rather they expose the wickedness, hidden behind the shadow of truth.

Those who listen with their eyes do not hear the vibration of Soul. Rather they deify the specter defining our mundane existence.

Those who behold with their nose cannot fathom the magnificence of human existence. Rather they serve to obscure the beauty of humanity by spurning the colors of light.

Those who try to touch fellow beings with their eyes cannot feel the vibration of human empathy. Rather they contaminate the vision by deflowering the yearnings of Soul.

Those who taste human species with ears cannot appreciate the swingeing aroma of civilization. Rather they define evolution in terms of mummies' silent interpretation of scriptures.

Those who don't understand the semantics of heart will find themselves dissolved into the fossils of sound. They can neither measure their existence nor can they fathom their Being.

It is the sozzled heart whence sprout truthful tantrums of Soul. Soul remains evermore thirsty for heart's inspiration.

I am on a mission to create new semantics of life.

My gospels are the most beautiful art ever engraved in the destiny of Time.

The ambience fraught with sinister political expediency cannot comprehend the sublime message of philosophy, poetry and arts.

I don't care whether or not I am in the right side of history. I just want to make sure that I am in the right side of my own conscience.

A little sparrow can peck an empire into pieces. This is what is known as the power of Soul.

Each soul finds its *femme fatale* in the eternal indifference of Time.

Hinduism believes in the Truth of Science, not in the political agendas of so-called scientists.

The more Science gets advanced, the more God will find Himself encouraged to tighten his grip over our process of thinking.

I don't think myself comparable to anyone in human society. I have never seen someone endowed with the impetuosity of wind, flow of a river, haughtiness of a mountain, insolence of a desert and moisture of dewdrops.

To me the sacred mantra OM represents at the same time the most celebrated apotheosis of philosophy and religion, literature and science, and emotion and intellect.

ABOUT THE AUTHOR

Ramesh Sharma is an impassioned advocate of the Upanishadic doctrine of 'Universality of Spirit'. He believes the US Constitution and the Declaration of Independence are profoundly influenced by the fundamental philosophy of Vedanta. To him, America's basic character as a nation is completely in sync with the principles of the Upanishads, the philosophical section of the Vedas. This conviction had inspired him to propose in his previous two books that America be formally declared a Hindu State. Interestingly, hard realities of human societies find their voice prudently echoed in his iconoclastic views about religion and philosophy.

Printed in the United States
By Bookmasters